100+ IDEA$ TO EARN MONEY ONLINE

100+ ACTIVE & PASSIVE INCOME STREAMS

VAIBHAV NALAWADE

Contents

Contents

Contents

Contents

Contents

100+ Ways To Earn $1000+

100+ Online Business Idea$

By Vaibhav Nalawade

Preface

Hello, if you are reading this eBook it means you are in search passive income then this eBook only for you. In this eBook you will 100+ business and job ideas that you can do form your home. Yes you can do this work from home.

Be your own Boss.

Foreword

Internet is everything, so why are you in office? Even if you can earn money from your home, as similar to your monthly salary. So, start working from home. You can start it without quitting Job and it will be passive income for you. And if you want to make fulltime in online ideas then do not quit your job until you dose not able to earn more money than your salary. Don't forget to read FAQs before reading this book. FAQs will be more helpful to read and understand easily.

Note: Please Check Last Page For All Useful Links

Data Entry Jobs

Data entry jobs are one of the simple ways to make money online. You have to convert an image file into a Word file by writing into it. There are many other types of data entry jobs available. You have to achieve an accuracy of over 99% and finish it on time. You should always look for legit data entry jobs because the market is full of scammers.

Skills: Computer Skills, Typing 30-40 WPM

Requirements: Computer or Laptop or Mobile and Internet

Cost: 0-500 For Internet

CHAPTER TWO

Online Focus Group

Companies like Google or Microsoft need feedback from their consumers about the product they are using. You can help them get feedback and in return, you get paid. Skills Requirements Investment Computer Skills, Communication and Product Testing skill Computer or Laptop or Mobile and Internet 0-500 For Internet.

Skills: Computer Skills, Communication, and Product Testing skills

Requirements: Computer or Laptop or Mobile and Internet

Investment: 0-500 For Internet

CHAPTER THREE

Online Tutoring

Websites like Tutor.com can help you find tutoring jobs. Here you are going to teach children online via Zoom, Google Meet, or other software. You can choose a subject that you know the best.

Skills: Computer Skills, any kind of knowledge that help to grow and SEO

Requirements: Computer or Laptop or Mobile, Internet, and camera

Investment: 0-500 For Internet

CHAPTER FOUR

Get Paid to Click

You can get paid to click on a link. This is called PTC or paid-to-click jobs. You just have to click a link and stay there for 2 to 3 minutes. You get paid a small amount for this particular task with Rozdhan.

Skills: Computer Skills

Requirements: Computer or Laptop or Mobile and Internet

Investment: 0-500 For Internet

CHAPTER FIVE

eBooks

Write eBooks and sell online. If you know about a particular subject like training your dog, cooking, music, or marketing then you can create an eBook and sell it online for $1 or $20 per copy as per your own valuation. You can Publish on Amazon Kindle with Amazon KDP

Skills: Computer Skills, Writting Skills

Requirements: Computer or Laptop or Mobile and Internet

Investment: 0-500 For Internet

CHAPTER SIX

Sharing Content

If you can create content that can go viral then you can make a lot of money. Your content will be shared around the internet and you will get paid. However, you have to create great content every time.

Skills: Computer Skills, Video Shooting Skills, Acting

Requirements: Computer or Laptop or Mobile and Internet

Investment: 0-500 For Internet

CHAPTER SEVEN

Surveys and Form Filling

There are various websites that offers you money for filling various survey forms. They pay according to number of surveys that you take. It takes 5 to 20 minutes to fill a form depending upon the survey. You get paid once you finish the survey.

Skills: Computer Skills

Requirements: Computer or Laptop or Mobile and Internet

Investment: 0-500 For Internet

CHAPTER EIGHT

Earn from Cashback Sites

Do you know you can make money each time you buy something from shopping sites like Amazon, eBay etc. You need to download apps or signup sites like CashKaro, Earnkaro etc. and then buy everything by clicking through these sites. You can get 2% to 5% of the amount of your total purchase as cashback from these sites

Skills: Computer Skills

Requirements: Computer or Laptop or Mobile and Internet

Investment: When you are buying any product then apply for cashback

Podcasting

Podcasting is booming and it will the future with in few years around 2022-23 you'll se every YouTuber will own his podcating channel. Podcasting is a great way to make money online. If you know about a subject like finance or current affairs then you can record videos and sell it online. People are ready to buy your podcast videos for few dollars. You can publish your podcast with Ancher.

Skills: Computer Skills

Requirements: Mic, Computer or Laptop or Mobile and Internet

Investment: 0-500 For Internet

CHAPTER TEN

Digital Or Online Journal

Digital journal is also like writing for an online version of a newspaper. However the difference is digital journal doesn't have any offline presence. You write columns as a web journalist.

Skills: Computer Skills, Writing Skills

Requirements: Computer or Laptop or Mobile and Internet

Investment: 0-500 For Internet

CHAPTER ELEVEN

Columnist for a Newspaper

You can write for an online version of a newspaper. You can write a column and get paid for each word you write. Online columnists are in great demand these days.

Skills: Computer Skills, Wrting Skills
Requirements: Computer or Laptop or Mobile and Internet
Investment: 0-500 For Internet

CHAPTER TWELVE

A Software, An App or A Web Solution

Finally, if you can come up with any kind of solution whether it is a kind of software or an app or a website then you can make a lot of money online. So these were 100+ ways to make money online. Are you using any of these ways? Share your method or experience of making money online. If you are not making money online yet, START NOW with one of the methods.

Skills: Computer Skills, Programming Skills, Web Design, Communication, UI & UX skills

Requirements: Computer or Laptop, code editor, android studio, MySQL, Java and Internet

Investment: 0-500 For Internet

CHAPTER THIRTEEN

Payment Gateway Web Solution

If you have expertise with coding then develop a web portal that is just like PayPal or Payoneer. You allow customers to transact money and you charge a fee on each transaction.

Skills: Computer Skills, Programming Skills, Web Design, Communication, UI & UX skills

Requirements: Computer or Laptop, code editor, android studio, MySQL, Java, and Internet

Investment: 0-500 For Internet

CHAPTER FOURTEEN

Mobile Recharge and Web to Mobile SMS Service

Create a web portal that allows recharging mobile phones and visitors can also send free SMS to someone else on their mobile. You will be the conduit between the network provider and customers.

Skills: Computer Skills, Programming Skills, Web Design, Communication, UI & UX skills

Requirements: Computer or Laptop, code editor, android studio, MySQL, Java, and Internet

Investment: 0-500 For Internet

CHAPTER FIFTEEN

Domain Name and Hosting Service

You start selling domain name and hosting service. There are many companies who sell domain name and hosting service. Start work with GoDaddy or Bluehost.

Skills: Computer Skills, Programming Skills, Web Design, Communication, UI & UX skills

Requirements: Computer or Laptop, Internet and Domain Names

Investment: 05K-20K For Domain Name

CHAPTER SIXTEEN

Network Blogging

You can establish a network of bloggers and make money by giving paid memberships who want to get inside the inner circle.

Skills: Computer Skills, Programming Skills, Web Design, Communication, UI & UX skills

Requirements: Computer or Laptop, code editor, android studio, MySQL, Java, and Internet

Investment: 0-500 For Internet

CHAPTER SEVENTEEN

Online MLM

If you are a network marketing leader & working with an MLM company then this is a great way to promote your MLM company online. There are very few people who know how to promote your MLM company on the internet and make huge money by recruiting hundreds of members under you.

Skills: Computer Skills

Requirements: Computer or Laptop, Internet, Web Hosting, Domain Name

Investment: 0-5000 For Internet, Domain Name, Hosting

CHAPTER EIGHTEEN

Direct TV

Not everyone can start a direct TV but if you can then there is a lot of money to be made here. You need some content to live broadcast it. You generate revenue through advertisements. But if you want to start with a low budget then start your YouTube channel with your TV name & be present on every social media platform.

Skills: Computer Skills, video editing, shooting, and acting

Requirements: Computer or Laptop, Internet, Web Hosting, Domain Name

Investment: 25K-10 Lac

CHAPTER NINETEEN

Answering Questions and Giving Advice

If you are live and active on forums and other Q & A platforms then you get paid for answering the right questions. But you need to have knowledge only then you can solve the problems of visitors. There are dozens of sites like KGB, Fun Advice, and Ether where you can signup and provide the right answers & advice to make money. You can do it on Quora and Chegg like websites.

Skills: Answer the quotations which skill already you have.

Requirements: Computer or Laptop or Mobile and Internet

Investment: 0-500 For Internet

CHAPTER TWENTY

Downloading Apps

If you download apps on your Smartphone and install them and use it for certain days then you get paid for it. There is a site called ChampCash and other android apps which pay you for downloading and installing apps on your phone. You can do it on Rozdhan and COinpop App

Skills: Mobile Operating

Requirements: Computer or Laptop or Mobile and Internet

Investment: 0-500 For Internet

CHAPTER TWENTY-ONE

Reward Sites – Bing, Listening Music

There are various reward sites like Bing which awards you with money if you listen music or click on a link. These reward sites pay you for various other things.

Skills: Computer Skills

Requirements: Computer or Laptop or Mobile and Internet

Investment: 0-500 For Internet

Ad Revenue System

You might have heard about Traffic Monsoon or Instamojo where you buy ad packs and make money when someone watches the ad. You invest dollars to make more dollars. If you are smart enough then you can make some money. However do not invest large amount of money because there is no guarantee of such sites. If you want to invest then go with Blogger or wordpress and free hosting.

Skills: Computer Skills, Programming Skills, Web Design, Communication, UI & UX skills

Requirements: Computer or Laptop, code editor, android studio, MySQL, Java, and Internet

Investment: 0-500 For Internet

CHAPTER TWENTY-THREE

Merchandize

Create Your own Merchandize and Sell Online In a nutshell you can create your own merchandise whether it is a mug or a t-shirt or a cap and sell it online. Start your shop on shopify.

Skills: Computer Skills, Programming Skills, Web Design, Communication, UI & UX skills

Requirements: Computer or Laptop, code editor, android studio, MySQL, Java, and Internet

Investment: 0-5K For Internet

CHAPTER TWENTY-FOUR

Sell Music and Videos

Sell Music and Videos If you have a good voice and can create great music then you can sell them online. You can also sell cute animal or baby videos online. You can service like Distrokid to sell music. And Shutterstock to sell video.

Skills: Computer Skills, video editing, shooting and acting and beats making

Requirements: Camera, Mic, Computer or Laptop or Mobile and Internet

Investment: 0-500 For Internet

CHAPTER TWENTY-FIVE

Arts and Crafts

Arts and Crafts Similarly you can sell other kinds of crafts which you make in your home but sell online. You do all the work from your home but sell it on sites like Etsy. Nowadays NFT is a craze you can create digital crafts.

Skills: Computer Skills, craftwork

Requirements: Computer or Laptop or Mobile and Internet

Investment: 3K-1 Lac

CHAPTER TWENTY-SIX

Art and Painting Auction

Art and Painting Auction If you collect arts and paintings then you can sell it online. If you have a passion for drawing paintings then you don't have to wait for an auction because you can anytime do it online.

Skills: Painting, Computer Skills

Requirements: Computer or Laptop or Mobile and Internet

Investment: 1K-10K

CHAPTER TWENTY-SEVEN

Stock Photography

Stock Photography Similarly in stock photography bloggers and other websites would like to buy photos from you for a cheaper rate. If you can take decent photos then you can turn it into a great business.

Skills: Photography, Computer Skills

Requirements: Camera, Computer or Laptop or Mobile and Internet

Investment: 0-500 For Internet

CHAPTER TWENTY-EIGHT

Sell Photos Online

Sell Photos Online Do you know your mobile camera can earn you good cash. Yes, if you a good photographer who can capture quality photos through your mobile camera or professional cameras then there are sites who are ready to pay you money for your photos. You can upload your photos on such photo sharing sites & earn money whenever someone buys your photo.

Skills: Photography, Computer Skills
Requirements: Camera, Computer or Laptop or Mobile and Internet
Investment: 0-500 For Internet

CHAPTER TWENTY-NINE

Make Money Selling Gadgets

Make Money Selling Gadgets You can sell your iPhone, laptop and other electronic gadgets online and make some money. You buy for a less price and sell it for more. So you make some profit. Start selling it on eBay.

Skills: Computer Skills

Requirements: Computer or Laptop or Mobile and Internet

Investment: 500-10K+ For Internet

CHAPTER THIRTY

Selling Courses Online

Selling courses Online You can design various courses in the form of eBooks or Podcasts and sell them online. You can become a vendor on Clickbank and take the help of other affiliate marketers there. These courses can be about cooking, how to start blogging, photography, etc. Their several sites to sell courses like Udemy

Skills: Computer Skills, Make Course On Where You're Expert.

Requirements: Computer or Laptop or Mobile and Internet

Investment: 0-500 For Internet

CHAPTER THIRTY-ONE

Selling Old Books Online

Selling Old Books Online If you have old books then you can visit a site like BookScouter where you can sell them for a few dollars. You have to enter the ISBN number and bid for the selling price. Sell books on eBay or Bookishsanta.

Skills: Computer Skills, Reading Habit
Requirements: Computer or Laptop or Mobile and Internet
Investment: 1K-20K

CHAPTER THIRTY-TWO

Peer to Peer Lending

Peer to Peer Lending, Peer to peer lending banks do not get involved in lending large loans. You as an individual can give or invest an amount and get returns on it. There are sites like Lending Club which take care of everything. You must know that person is a person capable to pay off the money that you lent to them. You can lend money 12Club app to a verified person.

Skills: Business Skills, Understanding Of Money
Requirements: Computer or Laptop or Mobile and Internet
Investment: 1K-50K+ For Internet

CHAPTER THIRTY-THREE

Stock Trading

Stock Trading You can trade stocks, commodities, and even mutual funds online. Just open an account with a broking firm and get started. Stock trading is not new however you must know about the markets otherwise you will lose money. You can invest money with any broker according to your countries like Drivewealth or INDMoney.

Skills: Finance Knowledge
Requirements: Computer or Laptop or Mobile and Internet
Investment: 10-500K+ For Internet

CHAPTER THIRTY-FOUR

Start Your Own Coupon Site

Start Your Own Coupon Site, Just like Amazon or eBay you can start your own coupon site. You will sell coupons on the behalf of merchants online. First, you make money with advertising, and later on, you can tie up with merchants and make money on commission. If you don't want to invest much then you can go with honey.

Skills: Computer Skills, Programming Skills, Web Design, Communication, UI & UX skills

Requirements: Computer or Laptop, Internet and Domain Names

Investment: 05K-20K For Domain Name

CHAPTER THIRTY-FIVE

Online University

An Online University You can create an online university and start giving certificates if you are certified. People will take courses from the online university and you will offer certificates. You charge money for every course. Like Upgrade.

Skills: Educational Knowledge.

Requirements: Computer or Laptop or Mobile and Internet

Investment: 0-500 For Internet

CHAPTER THIRTY-SIX

Resume Writing and Cover Writing

Resume Writing and Cover Writing, You can write resumes and design cover letters online. You get paid for writing and designing them. You can also make money if you can create PowerPoint presentations. You need to find such jobs online. Get work from Fiverr.

Skills: Writing Skills, Designing Skills & Computer Skills

Requirements: Computer or Laptop or Mobile and Internet

Investment: 0-500 For Internet

CHAPTER THIRTY-SEVEN

Captcha Writing

Captcha Writing You can write captcha online. You get paid for writing and solving them. You can also make money if you can fill forms only You need to find such jobs online.

Skills: Computer Skills

Requirements: Computer or Laptop or Mobile and Internet

Investment: 0-500 For Internet

CHAPTER THIRTY-EIGHT

Make Money Online with Simple Jobs

Make Money Online with Simple Jobs This is the first job I recommend to anyone who wants to make money online. Micro jobs are doing short tasks like reading emails, completing surveys, watching videos, writing comments, etc. Here are some of the most popular sites I can recommend to you for doing simple online jobs. Swagbux is – Best site if you are from the US, UK, Canada & good for everyone. ClixSense – One of the great & my favorite site.

Skills: Computer Skills

Requirements: Computer or Laptop or Mobile and Internet

Investment: 0-500 For Internet

CHAPTER THIRTY-NINE

Make Money Blogging

Make Money Blogging, If you want to make big money say above $1000 then blogging is the only simple, safe method that you can start. Although it may take some time initially, but trust me once you are an expert, there will be nothing like blogging that can give you time freedom and huge income both. Blog is nothing but a website where you write about your favourite topic on regular basis. You use some marketing techniques like SEO to get the traffic on your blog. As traffic starts coming, you can monetize your blog with Google AdSense program or affiliate. Passion for blogging and a hobby is must. Just check here some of the best resources that will help you to make money from blog. Start with zero investment with Blogger.

Skills: Computer Skills, Programming Skills, Web Design, Communication, UI & UX skills, Writing Skills

Requirements: Computer or Laptop, Internet and Domain Names

Investment: 0-20K For Domain Name

Freelance Gigs

Freelancing is the 2nd biggest opportunity on the internet where people make tons of money. On the internet, there are myriads of freelance gigs that you can find. There are dozens of popular freelance sites that offer you hundreds of different jobs that you can do for your clients. You can provide services like writing, web designing, data entry, virtual assistant, SEO, video maker, and graphic designing. Get work from fiverr.

Skills: Computer Skills

Requirements: Computer or Laptop or Mobile and Internet

Investment: 0-500 For Internet

CHAPTER FORTY-ONE

Google AdSense & Another Ad Network

Google AdSense & another ad network, Google is everything to me. I have made 90% of my total income either because of Google or directly from Google. Its more than 10 years, Google is regularly paying me monthly AdSense income. There is not a single month in the last 10 years when I did not receive income from Google AdSense. You must have a website or a blog to make money from AdSense. You can place AdSense ads on your website. People come to your website and when they click on any AdSense ads, Google pays you 68% of the amount they receive from their advertisers. And yes, you can even place ads from other ad networks like Google AdSense but I am sure, you will be dissatisfied. Here are some of the best resources that will help you with Google AdSense

Skills: Computer Skills, Programming Skills, Web Design, Communication, UI & UX skills, Writing Skills

Requirements: Computer or Laptop, Internet and Domain Names

Investment: 0-20K For Domain Name

CHAPTER FORTY-TWO

Make Money with Vlogging

Make Money with Vlogging, Vlogging or video blogging is where you create and upload great videos on YouTube or other video sharing sites. If your videos are special and people like it then you earn revenue by partnering with Google. Thousands of people are making good income running their own channel on YouTube. Here are some of the best resources to earn money online from YouTube.

Skills: Computer Skills, video editing, shooting, and acting

Requirements: Computer or Laptop, Internet, Web Hosting, Domain Name

Investment: 0K-10K Lac

CHAPTER FORTY-THREE

Network Affiliate Marketing

Network Affiliate Marketing, Network affiliate marketing is where you sell products on behalf of companies like Clickbank, Commission Junction, etc. Here you find thousands of vendors and you sell products on their behalf. It's always better for a beginner to work with an affiliate network because you can try a number of companies & their products from a single place & even get your earnings from all these companies in a single place. Like HerablLife.

Skills: Communication, Computer Skills

Requirements: Computer or Laptop or Mobile and Internet

Investment: 0-500 For Internet

CHAPTER FORTY-FOUR

Individual Affiliate Marketing

Individual Affiliate Marketing – HostGator, Bluehost, etc. Individual affiliate marketing is different than network affiliate marketing. Here you sell on behalf of one particular company. The money that you receive is paid by that company not a network like Clickbank or CJ. Here you get complete flexibility and the product matches the content of your blog. You can try big companies like Amazon, Flipkart, HostGator, AWeber, SEMRush, or anything related to your industry.

Skills: Computer Skills, Communication
Requirements: Computer or Laptop or Mobile and Internet
Investment: 0-500 For Internet

CHAPTER FORTY-FIVE

Make Money with URL Shortener

Make Money with URL Shortener, You can make money with URL shortener services like Google URL shortener or Bitly. You have to shorten an URL and distribute it online by various means. Once you get traffic and when visitors click on the link then you get paid for each click. You can use services like Shortus and shareus.

Skills: Computer Skills

Requirements: Computer or Laptop or Mobile and Internet

Investment: 0-500 For Internet

CHAPTER FORTY-SIX

Amazon or eBay Seller

Amazon or eBay Seller, The best way to start is to become a seller on e-commerce sites like Amazon and eBay where you can sell a lot of merchandise on their behalf. You easily earn a commission on each sale you make. It is very easy to get started however experience with marketing is very important. There are millions of sellers all over the world who make a full-time living selling various items on these sites.

Skills: Computer Skills, Digital Marketing

Requirements: Computer or Laptop or Mobile and Internet

Investment: 0-500 For Internet

Freelance Writing Work

Freelance Writing Work on Upwork, Elance, Fiverr etc Writing jobs that you can do online are copywriting, ghost writing, content writing etc. You can easily find writing jobs on Upwork, Fiverr, iWriter etc. You take a project and get paid by your hirer.

Skills: Computer Skills, writing skill

Requirements: Computer or Laptop or Mobile and Internet

Investment: 0-500 For Internet

CHAPTER FORTY-EIGHT

Writing Review

Writing Review. You get paid online for writing an honest review for movies, restaurants you eat at, or a place you visit. Companies and other third-party firms need you to write a review for them. You get work from test.com

Skills: Computer Skills, Reading Skills, Testing
Requirements: Computer or Laptop or Mobile and Internet
Investment: 0-500 For Internet

CHAPTER FORTY-NINE

Online Consultancy

Online Consultancy. This is best for people who have expertise in a particular field. Whether you are a teacher, doctor, feng shui expert, trainer, or anyone who has some skills that can solve the problems of others then you can start an online consultancy. You can promote your services through your blog, Google+, Facebook, etc. You can provide consultancy on phone or through Zoom or Google Meet.

Skills: Skills That You Can Provide Help, Communion

Requirements: Computer or Laptop or Mobile and Internet

Investment: 0-500 For Internet

CHAPTER FIFTY

Forex Trading

Forex Trading, Similarly, you can trade through Forex. However, in certain countries, forex trading is not allowed. You trade currency and make a huge amount of money and capital risk. You can for Forex Trading Apps Like Binance or OctaFX

Skills: Finance Knowledge

Requirements: Computer or Laptop or Mobile and Internet

Investment: 3K-500K+ For Capital

CHAPTER FIFTY-ONE

Sponsoring Links and Sponsored Post

Sponsoring Links and Sponsored Posts, You can sponsor links and posts on your website and make money with them. There are people who will be willing to pay you an amount if you allow them to sponsor their blog posts on your website.

Skills: Computer Skills, social media influencer, communication

Requirements: YouTube Channel,Computer or Laptop or Mobile and Internet

Investment: 0-500 For Internet

Paid or Sponsored Tweet

Paid or Sponsored Tweet, You can tweet on someone else behalf and make money. There are sites online which allow sponsored tweets.

Skills: Computer Skills, Writing Skills

Requirements: Twitter Account,Computer or Laptop or Mobile and Internet

Investment: 0-500 For Internet

CHAPTER FIFTY-THREE

Facebook Paid to Like

Facebook Paid to Like, You also get paid to like a Facebook page. Although such jobs are limited however you can find them online. But such jobs don't pay you much. But now days Facebook is loosing their subscribers so don't expect to much from Facebook.

Skills: Computer Skills

Requirements: Facebook Account,Computer or Laptop or Mobile and Internet

Investment: 0-500 For Internet

CHAPTER FIFTY-FOUR

Sign Up for a Credit Card

Sign Up for a Credit Card, There are many credit card companies that offer sign-up bonuses worth hundreds of dollars. You can sign up for such credit cards and make some money. Like Cred or UniPay.

Skills: Computer Skills

Requirements: Computer or Laptop or Mobile and Internet

Investment: 0-500 For Internet

CHAPTER FIFTY-FIVE

Earn with Mystery Shopping

Earn with Mystery Shopping, You shop on someone's behalf and send a report about the product and the service. You have to write a review on how well was a service in a given store. You get paid for writing honest reviews.

Skills: Computer Skills

Requirements: Computer or Laptop or Mobile and Internet

Investment: 1K-500K+ For Internet

CHAPTER FIFTY-SIX

Product Testing

Product Testing Companies around the world offer you money if you test their products and give a feedback. You have to use the product and send them a detailed feedback via an email. You get paid for the feedbacks. You get work from test.com

Skills: Computer Skills, Reading Skills, Testing
Requirements: Computer or Laptop or Mobile and Internet
Investment: 0-500 For Internet

Playing Online Games

Playing Online Games, You make money while playing games online. There are companies who develop online games and they need people who can play and test these games online. You get paid for playing games for certain hours. For extra income, you can also stream your game on YouTube.

Skills: Gaming Skills

Requirements: Computer or Laptop or Mobile and Internet

Investment: 0-500 For Internet

CHAPTER FIFTY-EIGHT

Online Beta Version Software Testing

Online Beta Version Software Testing Before releasing the website a company wants it to test it. Not just a website but other piece of software also. If you use the software and report on bugs or other code errors then you get paid for doing that.

You get work from test.com

Skills: Computer Skills, Reading Skills, Testing

Requirements: Computer or Laptop or Mobile and Internet

Investment: 0-500 For Internet

CHAPTER FIFTY-NINE

Crowdfunding

Crowdfunding, Crowdfunding is perhaps one of the most popular ways to make money online. You let people online donate money for you. However you have to have a nice story to pitch, only then people will donate money. You've to tell them how you're utilizing crowdfunded money.

Skills: Computer Skills, Communication
Requirements: Computer or Laptop or Mobile and Internet
Investment: 0-500 For Internet

CHAPTER SIXTY

Make Money with Webcam

Make Money with Webcam, You can record erotic videos and live telecast them using a webcam. You can charge money for each session and make a huge amount of money. You can go live on YouTube or Twitch while watching your Live Stream they will give you Superchat.

Skills: Computer Skills, Communication

Requirements: YouTube Channel,Computer or Laptop or Mobile and Internet

Investment: 0-500 For Internet

CHAPTER SIXTY-ONE

Raise Money for Charity

Raise Money for Charity, It may be unethical but you can make a lot of money through charity. If you have a cause and create a web page then you can attract people who are willing to donate money.

Skills: Communication Skills

Requirements: Computer or Laptop or Mobile and Internet

Investment: 0-500 For Internet

CHAPTER SIXTY-TWO

Travel and Cook Blog

Travel and Cook Blog and Show, If you have a passion for something like traveling or cooking then you can turn your hobby into blogging. You post great photos, videos, and your experience on regular basis on your blog. You will start receiving huge traffic. You can also upload videos on YouTube for additional income.

Skills: Computer Skills, Traveling, Cooking, Communication
Requirements: Computer or Laptop or Mobile and Internet
Investment: 5K-75K+

CHAPTER SIXTY-THREE

Selling Insurance Online

Selling Insurance Online, You can sell insurance on the behalf of insurance companies online. You will be like an agent who will sell insurance online. You need lots of contacts otherhand you can start your YouTube channel where you can explain about Insurance and sell them.

Skills: Communication Skills

Requirements: Computer or Laptop or Mobile and Internet

Investment: 0-500 For Internet

Sell Products On Your Own

Sell Products On Your Own – Garage Sale You can collect all the items that are catching dust in your garage and sell them online. You sell products and make money.

Skills: Computer Skills

Requirements: Computer or Laptop or Mobile and Internet

Investment: 10-500K+

CHAPTER SIXTY-FIVE

Web Services Development

Web Services Development, Growth of internet has allowed many startups to mushroom. These startups keep on innovating new business ideas. They come up with new solutions. You can create web services like software, apps or IT solutions for Internet users. You make huge money if an idea is successful. You also receive huge seed funding from various companies.

Skills: Computer Skills, Programming Skills, Web Design, Communication, UI & UX skills, Writing Skills

Requirements: Computer or Laptop, Internet and Domain Names

Investment: 0-20K For Domain Name

CHAPTER SIXTY-SIX

Ecommerce Site

Ecommerce Site, Ecommerce is picking up around the world. You can think of creating your own three tier website that sells merchandise. You don't have to be like Amazon but you can start selling your own products on your site. You can even check some of the local products that has huge demand but not available outside your locality. Another way is to tie up directly with manufacturer or distributer so that you can buy it for cheap & sell online with a margin through your website.

Skills: Computer Skills, Programming Skills, Web Design, Communication, UI & UX skills, Writing Skills

Requirements: Computer or Laptop, Internet and Domain Names

Investment: 0-20K For Domain Name

CHAPTER SIXTY-SEVEN

Real Estate Site

Real Estate Site, You can think of starting a real estate web portal. You will just be a conduit between the online visitor and the owner of a property. You make money when someone buys or rents a home online.

Skills: Computer Skills

Requirements: Computer or Laptop or Mobile and Internet

Investment: 10K-25K+

Reservation and Ticketing Portal

Reservation and Ticketing Portal, You can start hotel and air ticket booking web portal. These web portals receive huge traffic daily. You need to create a 3 tier website with front end, back end and a middleware.

Skills: Computer Skills, Programming Skills, Web Design, Communication, UI & UX skills, Writing Skills

Requirements: Computer or Laptop, Internet and Domain Names

Investment: 0-20K For Domain Name

CHAPTER SIXTY-NINE

Buying and Selling on Craigslist

Buying and Selling on Craigslist, Quikr etc You buy items on Craigslist, Quikr and other sites like craigslist and sell it there. You buy for cheaper rates and sell it at a much higher rates. However in order to do that you need to have some experience about selling stuff online.

Skills: Computer Skills

Requirements: Computer or Laptop or Mobile and Internet

Investment: 2K-10K+

CHAPTER SEVENTY

Vehicle Review

Car/Bike Review/Comparison Portal Car selling portal is also very popular. Lots of people are coming online for looking for a new car models. They want to check review or compare cars/bikes. If you can attract them on your website then you can make a lot of money just by advertising.

Skills: Vehicle Knowledge

Requirements: Computer or Laptop or Mobile and Internet

Investment: 10K+

Installing Auto Responder

Installing Auto Responder, like Aweber and Collecting Email List If you have an expertise for developing an auto responder like Aweber then you can make millions of dollars every month. You are renting your service for a fee every month. However for coding and developing the software you need to have a team.

Skills: Computer Skills, Programming Skills, Web Design, Communication, UI & UX skills, Writing Skills

Requirements: Computer or Laptop, Internet and Domain Names

Investment: 0-20K For Domain Name

CHAPTER SEVENTY-TWO

Online Ad and Branding Agencies

Online Ad and Branding Agencies, Online advertising and branding agencies have a great future. As the reach of the internet expands you will find companies reaching out to customers online. Hence they will need online advertising and branding agencies to develop their brand. If you are in advertising and branding business then think of starting an online agency.

Skills: Digital Marketing, SEO, Ad Handling, Computer Skills, Programming Skills, Web Design, Communication, UI & UX skills, Writing Skills

Requirements: Computer or Laptop, Internet and Domain Names

Investment: 0-20K For Domain Name

CHAPTER SEVENTY-THREE

SEO Services

SEO Services, SEO or search engine services are very hot. There are number of companies which are looking for a SEO expert that can rank their website high on the Google. If you have experience and know everything about SEO then go for it. You can either start an SEO business or provide freelance services.

Skills: Computer Skills, Web Development Knowledge, Keywords Ranking, Digital Marketing

Requirements: Computer or Laptop or Mobile and Internet

Investment: 0-500 For Internet

CHAPTER SEVENTY-FOUR

Search Engine Marketing

SEM, SEM or Search engine marketing is extension of SEO. Here you focus on SEO plus marketing. These two online jobs are very hot right now and you can make a lot of money with it. Here you must be an expert in Google AdWords, Facebook ads, Bing ads etc. People can pay you 10% to 20% of the advertising budget.

Skills: Computer Skills, Web Development Knowledge, Keywords Ranking, Digital Marketing

Requirements: Computer or Laptop or Mobile and Internet

Investment: 0-500 For Internet

CHAPTER SEVENTY-FIVE

Newsletter Marketing

Newsletter Marketing Here you bombard your client with newsletters daily. Either they subscribed to you or you send them newsletters daily. You attach a sales pitch with the newsletter. You have to know the exact demographics of your client before you market a product.

Skills: Computer Skills, Writting Skills

Requirements: Computer or Laptop or Mobile and Internet

Investment: 0-500 For Internet

Email Marketing

Email marketing is also like newsletter marketing however here you send your clients a sales letter via email. You send thousands of emails to a list of people and convert them into future prospects. You can get emails from sevrel sites like emailsdata.

Skills: Writing Skills, Communication, Computer Skills
Requirements: Computer or Laptop or Mobile and Internet
Investment: 0-500 For Internet

CHAPTER SEVENTY-SEVEN

Email list or Database Selling

Email list or Database Selling, This is quite different from the previous two. Here you sell an email list to marketers. You have to have a database of thousands of people that you are going to sell to marketers online. However, the database must be fresh and relevant otherwise no one would buy it.

Skills: Contacts, Computer Skills

Requirements: Computer or Laptop or Mobile and Internet

Investment: 0-500 For Internet

CHAPTER SEVENTY-EIGHT

Online HR Recruiting

Online HR Recruiting, Today after the advent of social media most of the recruiting is done online. If you are an HR recruiter then you can find candidates through LinkedIn and refer them to your client. However you must have a decent profile with dozens of HRs in your social network.

Skills: Communication

Requirements: Computer or Laptop or Mobile and Internet

Investment: 0-500 For Internet

CHAPTER SEVENTY-NINE

Social Media Marketing

Social Media Marketing, Social media can be used for marketing if you are familiar with Facebook, Twitter, or YouTube. You can be a marketer that targets only social media. Companies are in great need of social media marketers. Now this will be crazy around 2023 everyone will be on social media and if they want a social media presence you contact them.

Skills: Communication, Designing, Computer Skills, Photoshop
Requirements: Computer or Laptop or Mobile and Internet
Investment: 0-500 For Internet

CHAPTER EIGHTY

Social Media Executive

Social Media Executive / Manager Similarly companies also need social media managers to manage their operations on Facebook, Twitter, YouTube, etc. You must have experience with social media platforms like Facebook where you can run a campaign for the company you are working with. There is also a great scope for handling the Twitter account of celebrities, companies, or other big personalities where you will tweet on their behalf & manage the followers and responses.

Skills: Communication, Designing, Computer Skills, Photoshop
Requirements: Computer or Laptop or Mobile and Internet
Investment: 0-500 For Internet

Online PR

Online PR. Firm Earlier Public Relations were limited to TV and newspaper. However now online is also a major platform for PR. If you have experience with PR then you start promoting people online and charge a fee.

Skills: Computer Skills, Acting, Communication

Requirements: Computer or Laptop or Mobile and Internet

Investment: 0-500 For Internet

CHAPTER EIGHTY-TWO

WordPress Plugins

WordPress Plugins, There are companies who want to hire or outsource their website designing tasks to people who know to work with WordPress themes and plugins. You also add some code to it and deliver the website to your clients. You can publish your WordPress plugins on the WordPress store.

Skills: Computer Skills, Programming Skills, Web Design, Communication, UI & UX skills, Digital Marketing Skills

Requirements: Computer or Laptop, Internet and Domain Names

Investment: 0-2K

Website Flipping

Website Flipping, Just like domain flipping, there is great potential in another similar business and that is website flipping. Here you don't sell a domain but a complete website. But in order to earn online, your website must be a quality website with good traffic & at least 6 months of earning history. Here you buy a domain, write regular content & promote your website through social media and SEO & once you get the traffic & make some money, you can sell it. There are sites like Flippa and Empire Flippers which can help you out by getting 10-20 times the price of your monthly earnings. You can also buy websites from the above platforms, work on the site to grow traffic & income, and then sell it at a higher price.

Skills: Computer Skills, Programming Skills, Web Design, Communication, UI & UX skills, Digital Marketing Skills

Requirements: Computer or Laptop, Internet and Domain Names

Investment: 2K-10K+

Domain Flipping

Domain Flipping, Domain buying and selling can make you rich overnight. You buy a domain with a right name. You don't use it but just keep it with you and sell to a bigger player for a higher rate. You can sell 10 to 20 times higher of your buying price. Sometime your domain might fetch you thousands of dollars. If you don't believe, you can check this list of most expensive domains. You need to do lots of research & must have experience before you make 10 to 50 times from your purchased domains

Skills: Computer Skills, Programming Skills, Web Design, Communication, Digital Marketing Skills

Requirements: Computer or Laptop, Internet and Domain Names

Investment: 2K-10K+

CHAPTER EIGHTY-FIVE

Contextual Advertising

Contextual Advertising, Infolink If your blog is getting some traffic then you can monetize it with contextual advertising and info links. You get paid for showing ads and anchor texts that contains a link.

Skills: Computer Skills

Requirements: Computer or Laptop or Mobile and Internet

Investment: 0-500 For Internet

CHAPTER EIGHTY-SIX

Visual Arts

Visual Arts and Designing. Jobs If you know about designing then you can find jobs on websites like 99 designs or Envato Studio. These sites have a huge number of members who are making money by designing various cover of magazines and online publications.

Skills: Photoshop, Color Understanding, Graphic Design, Computer Skills

Requirements: Computer or Laptop or Mobile and Internet

Investment: 0-500 For Internet

Online Journalism

Online journalism or web journalism is nothing new and it is getting better day by day. You write for an online version of cable TV news network. You work with their web desk.

Skills: Communication, Computer Skills

Requirements: Computer or Laptop or Mobile and Internet

Investment: 0-500 For Internet

CHAPTER EIGHTY-EIGHT

Task Apps

Phone Apps There are various smartphone applications that pay you if you perform certain tasks. If you shop using an app then they pay you once you have completed a task. Like Taskbucks.

Skills: Computer Skills

Requirements: Computer or Laptop or Mobile and Internet

Investment: 0-500 For Internet

CHAPTER EIGHTY-NINE

Shared Hosting

Giving Space to Publishing On Your Website If your blog or website is very popular and getting huge traffic then you can sell some space of your site for marketing. You can set a price for showing ads on your website.

Skills: Computer Skills, Programming Skills, Web Design, Communication, UI & UX skills, Digital Marketing Skills

Requirements: Computer or Laptop, Internet and Domain Names

Investment: 2K-10K+

CHAPTER NINETY

Membership Sites,

Membership Sites, Similarly, you can create a site that solves a particular problem that people are looking for. Later on as traffic increases you can start charging for becoming a member so they can access more serious content. Creating a membership is very easy through WordPress. Either you can buy a theme or plugin to make your site as membership site.

Skills: Computer Skills, Programming Skills, Web Design, Communication, UI & UX skills, Digital Marketing Skills

Requirements: Computer or Laptop, Internet and Domain Names

Investment: 2K-10K+

CHAPTER NINETY-ONE

Revenue Sharing Sites

Revenue Sharing Sites, If you have something to share with the world, then there are many sites where you can write your expertise or experience and make money through Google AdSense or affiliate programs. You need to learn little bit about keyword research and SEO so that you can apply this on your written post and get more traffic.

Skills: Payment Gateway, Computer Skills, Programming Skills, Web Design, Communication, UI & UX skills, Digital Marketing Skills

Requirements: Computer or Laptop, Internet and Domain Names

Investment: 2K-10K+

Ghost Writing

Write for other sites Can't have your own blog then you can write for some other established sites or bloggers on the internet. You can contact them in person and decide on rates for each blog post you write. Your writing quality must be exceptional if you want to make big money from this. There are sites that can pay you up to $200 for each post.

Skills: Writing, Copy Writing, Computer Skills
Requirements: Computer or Laptop or Mobile and Internet
Investment: 0-500 For Internet

CPA

CPA, CPA or cost per action allows you to pay if you get people to sign up or register for a website. Here commissions can be great. Like Pekoworkers.

Skills: Computer Skills

Requirements: Computer or Laptop or Mobile and Internet

Investment: 0-500 For Internet

Cover Desiging

Cover Publishing You can design publications, and the front pages of magazines online by using adobe Photoshop. You can sell your design online.

Skills: Photoshop, Computer Skills
Requirements: Computer or Laptop or Mobile and Internet
Investment: 0-500 For Internet

Coding Services

Coding Services, You will never run out of clients if you know about coding. Coding jobs are not rare however you must know how to code. You have to write codes for fixing a given problem or designing a functionality of a website. The money is also great here.

Skills: Programming Language, Testing, Web Development, Computer Skills

Requirements: Computer or Laptop or Mobile and Internet

Investment: 0-500 For Internet

CHAPTER NINETY-SIX

Web Designing with PHP

Web Designing with PHP, Web designing with PHP or ASP will be quite different than setting up WordPress code or plug-in. Here you will design fully fledged website with a backend database. You may also require having a team with coders, designers and testers.

Skills: PHP, HTML, MySqlComputer Skills

Requirements: Computer or Laptop or Mobile and Internet

Investment: 0-500 For Internet

CHAPTER NINETY-SEVEN

Developing Mobile Apps

Developing Mobile Apps App development for Android or iOS devices has always been a lucrative business. If you can develop an innovative app that solves people's problems then you can make huge money with it. However, you have to have experience with coding. You can also get the business from companies & individuals to develop a customized application for their business or services.

Skills: Java, XML, SQLite, Firebase, Flutter, Computer Skills

Requirements: Computer or Laptop or Mobile and Internet

Investment: 0-500 For Internet

CHAPTER NINETY-EIGHT

Transcription Transcription jobs are readily available online. You have to copy and write from one medium to another. Most of the time you will find medical transcription jobs that pays you well.

Skills: Writing, Computer Skills

Requirements: Computer or Laptop or Mobile and Internet

Investment: 0-500 For Internet

Translating

Translating, You can also find translating jobs where you will be translating from one language to another. Translating jobs are fewer in number than transcription jobs. However still you can find few translating jobs online.

Skills: Knowledge Of Multi Language, Computer Skills
Requirements: Computer or Laptop or Mobile and Internet
Investment: 0-500 For Internet

Tech Support

Tech Support, Big corporations outsource their customer support to others. You can find tech support jobs online where you have to solve technology-related problems. These problems can be issues related to computer hardware or software. You can create a YouTube channel also for it.

Skills: Product Knowledge, Communication, Computer Skills
Requirements: Computer or Laptop or Mobile and Internet
Investment: 0-500 For Internet

CHAPTER ONE HUNDRED AND ONE

Web Assistant or Virtual Assistant You can make money online by becoming virtual assistant. Here your job we will be taking care of all the meetings and presentations that are to be held on a given date. Throught Zoom or Google Meet you can connect with your clients.

Skills: Computer Skills

Requirements: Computer or Laptop or Mobile and Internet

Investment: 0-500 For Internet

Instagram Paid Post

Instagram Paid Post, You can make money online by becoming an Instagram influencer. If you have followers then you can make paid posts and also share there product in stories. This is currently a trending earning source.

Skills: Grahic Design, Computer Skills

Requirements: Insta Followers At Leat 5K

Investment: 0-500 For Internet

WhatsApp Marketing

WhatsApp Marketing, You can also earn money on WhatsApp by sharing your products. And also you can convenes them to join your MLM network. Here conversion rate is very high. You can use brodcasting tools for sending messeges.

Skills: Contacts, Computer Skills
Requirements: Computer or Laptop or Mobile and Internet
Investment: 0-500 For Internet

Telegram Channel

Telegram channel is also similar to WhatsApp group. And you get more features in the telegram Channel. Like you can add up to 200 people to your channel. And more than 2 Lac+ people can join your channel. You make sponsored posts on your channel. Even you can create paid channels also.

Skills: Computer Skills

Requirements: Computer or Laptop or Mobile and Internet

Investment: 0-500 For Internet

Utopia Mining

Utopia Mining, Utopia is new in the market and it will future because it decentralized Internet server. It means it does not store any information on its server. It stores all data on your hard disk. And it is Peer to Peer network. By using this mining software you can earn money by mining.

Skills: Computer Skills

Requirements: Computer or Laptop or Mobile and Internet

Investment: 0-500 For Internet

Other Mining

Other Mining You can also mine in other currencies like Ethereum, Bitcoin, Doges and many other mining tools you can use to mining. Eg. Bitcoin through Honeyminer,

Skills: Computer Skills

Requirements: Computer or Laptop or Mobile and Internet

Investment: 0-500 For Internet

Consultant For Farmer

Consultant For Farmer This is brand new concept no one doing this right now. You can support farmers by providing information that they want. And you have required strong studies of farming. Eg. Bijak. This huge gap in market.

Skills: Farming Knowledge, Computer Skills
Requirements: Computer or Laptop or Mobile and Internet
Investment: 0-500 For Internet

ED-Tech StartUp

ED-Tech StartUp You can start your own online course by providing an app or website. Give a platform to share courses on your platform you can charge some percentages of the course fee. Note that you don't have to create any courses. E.g. Unacademy, Udemy

Skills: Web Development, Computer Skills

Requirements: Computer or Laptop or Mobile and Internet

Investment: 0-500 For Internet

Innovate New Ideas

Innovate New Ideas Problem is a solution and a solution is a new Idea. Just write down all problems that you encountered before and that you are facing in the future. If any problem that you can crack then work on it. Or you can share or sell your idea to someone.

Skills: Creative Thinking, Computer Skills
Requirements: Computer or Laptop or Mobile and Internet
Investment: 0-500 For Internet

Sell Licence Of Software

Sell Licence Of Software, You can sell your software online. Like management software for hotels or any other shop. You can charge yearly fees to your costumer. You can make it standalone it will be more helpful. You can do this even through YouTube Channel.

Skills: Computer Skills

Requirements: Computer or Laptop or Mobile and Internet

Investment: 0-500 For Internet

Online Finance Adviser

Online Finance Adviser, You can also become a Finance adviser for any person or for any company in your free time. Initially, you can work for any company part-time. Because they give training to you free of cost. And after that, you can give your service to any person full-time. This includes lots of risks so be careful.

Skills: Finance Knowledge, Computer Skills
Requirements: Computer or Laptop or Mobile and Internet
Investment: 0-500 For Internet

Share Market Broker

Share Market Broker, You can also become a Share Market Broker for companies. You can earn a brokerage charge by joining people for a Demat account. Share market broker Campines give you up to 10% of brokerage charge and some commission. You can up to 2500 per account opening like upstox.

Skills: Finance Knowledge, Computer Skills

Requirements: Computer or Laptop or Mobile and Internet

Investment: 0-500 For Internet

Amazon Delivery Guy

Amazon Delivery Guy, You can work as an amazon delivery guy part-time. By working 1-2 hours daily you can earn up to 400 rupees per day. You can work on your flexible time. You can get this job from awigan app.

Skills: Driving Skills

Requirements: Computer or Laptop or Mobile and Internet

Investment: 0-500 For Internet

Verify Business

Verify Business On Google Map You can earn money by helping to verify business account on google map. If account is not verify google does not recommend your business in search. So you can find unverified account and verify them. You can charge up to 7000 rupees per account.

Skills: Communication, Computer Skills

Requirements: Computer or Laptop or Mobile and Internet

Investment: 0-500 For Internet

Online Reputation Manager

Online Reputation Manager Online Reputation is going big thing in the next few years because Internet use increasing day by day. Famous Celebrities and products will get negative publicity then you should make this clear is this a genuine review or to spread negativity if genuine then work on it. And if this for to spread negativity then remove this content or in case be ready to file Lawsuit.

Skills: Communication, Computer Skills
Requirements: Computer or Laptop or Mobile and Internet
Investment: 0-500 For Internet

Food Reviews

Food Reviews You can get a food review job for Swiggy and Zamato. You have to secretly visit Swiggy or Zamato restaurants and test their food and service quality. If you found report it. You can do this on your weekend because it will be like your picnic.

Skills: Foody, Food Test, Skills

Requirements: Computer or Laptop or Mobile and Internet

Investment: 0-500 For Internet

Online Vegetable App

Online Vegetable App Now everyone wants to buy everything online. The E-commerce sector becoming more competitive. So you can start your vegetable delivery app. You can deliver vegetables in every 3-4 days.

Skills: Android App Development, Computer Skills

Requirements: Computer or Laptop or Mobile and Internet

Investment: 0-500 For Internet

Online Repairing

Online Mobile And Laptop Repairing Nowadays on average in every 15 days companies lunch new mobile. You can tap this market by providing them online repairing service.

Skills: Mobile & Laptop Repairing, Computer Skills

Requirements: Computer or Laptop or Mobile and Internet

Investment: 0-500 For Internet

All Service Providers

All Service Providers Contacts You can collect contacts of service providers and share them with those who want them on your website. You can monetize your website or take some money to enroll their contact on your website. You can do both. Like JustDail.

Skills: Web Development, Computer Skills

Requirements: Computer or Laptop or Mobile and Internet

Investment: 0-500 For Internet

Online Meditation Club

Online Meditation Club You can start your Meditation club online using website or app. Initially you start it on YouTube Channel and after you can sell them your premium content. You can do it live on YouTube or make paid meeting on Zoom.

Skills: Meditation, Yoga, Computer Skills
Requirements: Computer or Laptop or Mobile and Internet
Investment: 0-500 For Internet

Webinar

Webinar is online seminar. You can showcase your skills through webinar and you can charge some amount of money. And value in their life. On zoom.

Skills: Computer Skills

Requirements: Computer or Laptop or Mobile and Internet

Investment: 0-500 For Internet

Whatsapp Newsletter

Whatsapp Newsletter, You can start a WhatsApp newsletter or news channel on WhatsApp using broadcast. LetsUp is the best example of it.y Their are several tools to broadcast tools to send newsletter and send ads with them.

Skills: Contacts, Computer Skills

Requirements: Computer or Laptop or Mobile and Internet

Investment: 0-500 For Internet

Sell Course on WhatsApp

Sell Course on WhatsApp, You can sell your skills in course and you can publish it on WhatsApp. Or you can take classes tgrouh whatsapp. You can do this automatic with Razorpay & Pabbly connect.

Skills: Computer Skills

Requirements: Computer or Laptop or Mobile and Internet

Investment: 0-500 For Internet

Faqs

xx+ Amount means you have to at least xx money or more.

0-xx+ It means if you want to improve your service then you can invest more.

Computer Skills contains writing, typing, good communication.

Till you have any queries You Can DM Me On Instagram @vaibhavnalawade7

Note: We(I) are not responsible for any kind of profit or loss to by using this ebook or book. To invest money in this idea(s) is your decision and you're responsible for it. Scan This QR Code For All Links That You Can Earn Money.

Get Links Now

Thank You

Thanks! If your facing any problem then you can DM (Direct Message) on Instagram to Author.

Also you can Follow Author, You don't have to But you can Follow To Author on Instagram.

Instagram Username: @vaibhavnalawade7

Author's Profile Link: https://instagram.com/vaibhavnalawade7